Reversible

Scrap Afghans

with the Double-Ended Crochet Hook

Bobbie Matela, Managing Editor
Carol Wilson Mansfield, Art Director
Mary Ann Frits, Editorial Director
Kathy Wesley, Senior Editor
Denise Black, Pattern Editor
Stephanie Hill and Sandy Scoville, Editorial Staff
Deborah Michael, Graphic Designer

**For a full-color catalog including books of
crochet designs, write to:**

American School of Needlework
Consumer Division
**1455 Linda Vista Drive
San Marcos, CA 92069**

or visit us at: http://www.asnpub.com

Shown on front cover: Stained Glass

Patterns tested and models made by Denise Black, Darla J. Fanton, Carly Poggemeyer, Kelly Robinson, and Darlene M. Wheeler

We have made every effort to ensure the accuracy and completeness of these instructions. We cannot, however, be responsible for human error, typographical mistakes, or variations in individual work.

Introduction

Using the popular Crochet on the Double™ hook technique Darla Fanton has created five innovative scrap afghan designs that are fun to crochet. And as a special bonus, all of these afghans are reversible!

Each afghan uses no more than one skein of each yarn color with additional skeins needed of one main color. From the colorful *Scrappy Squares* and *Aurora Stripings* to the striking *Stained Glass* and *Fiesta Fantasy*, you'll enjoy creating these beauties while using up odd skeins of yarn left over from other projects. Darla has even included *Colors for Baby* for the next baby shower.

If you haven't tried Crochet on the Double™ before, we've included basic instructions for crocheting with the double-ended hook.

Contents

Stitch Review

Reversible Crochet with the Double-Ended Hook

To review, you'll need:
One Size K Double-Ended Hook
Worsted Weight Yarn: 1 skein each of two contrasting
    colors
Note: A double-ended hook is held like a knife with
    your index finger on top for maximum control.

METHOD I – Using Vertical Bars

Foundation Row:
Step 1: With Color A, and using either end of hook, ch 12.

Step 2: Working in BL only of each ch, draw up a lp in
2nd ch from hook and in each rem ch **(Photo 1)**, leaving each lp on hook—12 lps of Color A now on hook.

Photo 1

Slide all lps to opposite end of hook and turn work in
direction shown by arrow **(Photo 2)**.

Photo 2

Pattern Row 1:
Step 1: To left of work, make a sl knot on hook with
Color B; draw sl knot through first lp of Color A now
on hook **(Photo 3)**; you now have one lp of Color B
and 11 lps of Color A on hook.

Photo 3

Step 2: † YO and draw through both Color B lp and
next Color A lp **(Photo 4)** †—10 Color A lps rem; working from left to right, rep from † to † across row; one
Color B lp will rem on hook.

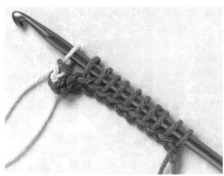

Photo 4

Look at your work. You will see that after Step 2 is completed, there is a row of Color A vertical bars **(Photo 5)**,
which count as stitches. DO NOT TURN WORK.

Photo 5

Pattern Row 2:
Continuing with Color B, sk first vertical bar; working
from right to left, † insert hook from right to left
UNDER next vertical bar **(Photo 6)** and draw up a
lp †; rep from † to † under each rem bar, leaving all
lps on hook–12 lps of Color B. Slide work to opposite
end of hook and turn.

Photo 6

*Hint: Work is turned only when all lps rem on hook;
when just one lp rems on hook, work is not turned.*

Alternating colors, rep Pattern Rows 1 and 2, except at beginning of Row 1 you will not need to make a slip knot, as new yarn color will already be in position to be used.

Repeat Pattern Rows 1 and 2 until you feel comfortable working the stitch. End by working Row 1.

Last Row:
Sk first vertical bar, ***** insert hook under next vertical bar; YO and draw through both lps on hook **(Photo 7)**; rep from ***** across row. At end, finish off.

Photo 7

METHOD II – Using Horizontal Bars
This method differs only slightly from Method 1, but gives a lighter, more open fabric.

To practice, work as for Method I through Step 2 of Pattern Row 1.

Again look at your work; you are familiar with the vertical bars; note that between sts there are also horizontal bars **(Photo 8)**.

Photo 8

Pattern Row 2:
Sk first vertical bar; † insert hook from front to back under next horizontal bar **(Photo 9)** and draw up a lp †; leaving all lps on hook, rep from † to † across row—12 lps.

Photo 9

Continue as for Method 1, repeating until you feel confident working this way.

An Important Word About Gauge

A correct stitch gauge is very important. Please take the time to work a stitch gauge swatch about 4" x 4". Measure the swatch. If the number of stitches and rows are fewer than indicated under "Gauge" in the pattern, your hook is too large. Try another swatch with a smaller size hook. If the number of stitches and rows are more than indicated under "Gauge" in the pattern, your hook is too small. Try another swatch with a larger size hook.

Keeping Stitches on Double-Ended Hooks

When working a wide piece with many stitches, a double-ended hook with a flexible center cable will allow you to work without fear of stitches slipping off the hook. These cabled hooks are especially recommended for full-size afghans and throws. They are also convenient for baby afghans, although the 14"-long double-ended hooks will work.

When using 14" double-ended hooks, it is helpful to place a point protector on the non-working end. Since point protectors are designed for knitting needles, you will find them with knitting notions in your needlework department.

If you cannot find these items, contact the publisher for a source.

Abbreviations and Symbols

beg.	begin(ning)
BL(s)	back loop(s)
ch(s)	chain(s)
gm(s)	gram(s)
lp(s)	loop(s)
oz	ounce(s)
patt	pattern
prev	previous
rem	remain(ing)
rep	repeat(ing)
rnd(s)	round(s)
sc	single crochet(s)
sk	skip
sl	slip
sl st(s)	slip stitch(es)
sp(s)	space(s)
st(s)	stitch(es)
tog	together
yd(s)	yard(s)
YO	yarn over

* An asterisk is used to mark the beginning of a portion of instructions to be worked more than once; thus, "rep from * twice more" means after working the instructions once, repeat the instructions following the asterisk twice more (3 times in all).

† The dagger identifies a portion of instructions that will be repeated again later in the same row or round.

— The number after a long dash at the end of a row or round indicates the number of stitches you should have when the row or round has been completed. The long dash can also be used to indicate a completed stitch such as a decrease, a shell, or a cluster.

() Parentheses are used to enclose instructions which should be worked the exact number of times specified immediately following the parentheses, such as "(2 sc in next dc, sc in next dc) twice." They are also used to set off and clarify a group of stitches that are to be worked all into the same space or stitch, such as "in next corner sp work (2 dc, ch 1, 2 dc)."

[] Brackets and () parentheses are used to provide additional information to clarify instructions.

Join - join with a sl st unless otherwise specified.

Fringe

Basic Instructions
Cut a piece of cardboard half as long as specified in instructions for strands plus ½" for trimming allowance. Wind yarn loosely and evenly lengthwise around cardboard. When cardboard is filled, cut yarn across one end. Do this several times, then begin fringing; you can wind additional strands as you need them.

Single Knot Fringe
Hold specified number of strands for one knot of fringe together, then fold in half. Hold afghan with right side facing you. Use crochet hook to draw folded end through space or stitch from right to wrong side (**Figs 1** and **2**), pull loose ends through folded section (**Fig 3**) and draw knot up firmly (**Fig 4**). Space knots as indicated in pattern instructions.

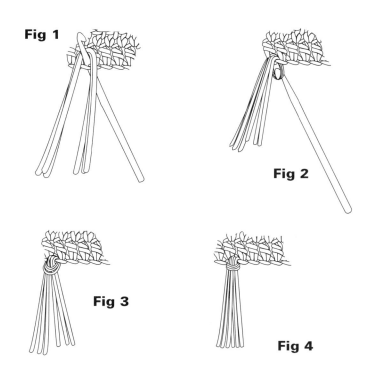

Fig 1

Fig 2

Fig 3

Fig 4

Stitch Guide

Chain - ch:
YO, draw through lp on hook.

Single Crochet - sc:
Insert hook in st, YO and draw through, YO and draw through both lps on hook.

Half Double Crochet - hdc:
YO, insert hook in st, YO, draw through, YO and draw through all 3 lps on hook.

Double Crochet - dc:
YO, insert hook in st, YO, draw through, (YO and draw through 2 lps on hook) twice.

Triple Crochet - trc:
YO twice, insert hook in st, YO, draw through, (YO and draw through 2 lps on hook) 3 times.

Slip Stitch - sl st:
(a) Used for Joinings
Insert hook in indicated st, YO and draw through st and lp on hook.

(b) Used for Moving Yarn Over
Insert hook in st, YO draw through st and lp on hook.

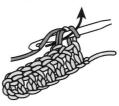

Front Loop - FL:
The front loop is the loop toward you at the top of the stitch.
Back Loop - BL:
The back loop is the loop away from you at the top of the stitch.
Post:
The post is the vertical part of the stitch.

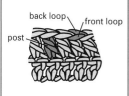

Overcast Stitch is worked loosely to join crochet pieces.

Metric Conversion Charts

INCHES INTO MILLIMETERS & CENTIMETERS (Rounded off slightly)

inches	mm	cm	inches	cm	inches	cm	inches	cm
1/8	3		5	12.5	21	53.5	38	96.5
1/4	6		5 1/2	14	22	56	39	99
3/8	10	1	6	15	23	58.5	40	101.5
1/2	13	1.3	7	18	24	61	41	104
5/8	15	1.5	8	20.5	25	63.5	42	106.5
3/4	20	2	9	23	26	66	43	109
7/8	22	2.2	10	25.5	27	68.5	44	112
1	25	2.5	11	28	28	71	45	114.5
1 1/4	32	3.2	12	30.5	29	73.5	46	117
1 1/2	38	3.8	13	33	30	76	47	119.5
1 3/4	45	4.5	14	35.5	31	79	48	122
2	50	5	15	38	32	81.5	49	124.5
2 1/2	65	6.5	16	40.5	33	84	50	127
3	75	7.5	17	43	34	86.5		
3 1/2	90	9	18	46	35	89		
4	100	10	19	48.5	36	91.5		
4 1/2	115	11.5	20	51	37	94		

CROCHET HOOKS CONVERSION CHART

U.S.	1/B	2/C	3/D	4/E	5/F	6/G	8/H	9/I	10/J	10 1/2/K	N
Continental-mm	2.25	2.75	3.25	3.5	3.75	4.25	5	5.5	6	6.5	9.0

Stained Glass

Size:
About 45" x 60" without fringe

Materials:
Worsted weight yarn, 34 oz (2380 yds, 1020 gms) M/C; 32 oz (2240 yds, 960 gms) scraps

Note: *Our photographed afghan was made with 34 oz (2380 yds, 1020 gms) black (M/C) and less than one skein each of 10 different colors.*

Size H (5mm) double-ended crochet hook or size required for gauge

Size 16 tapestry needle

Gauge:
4 sts= 1"

Instructions

Notes: *When beginning and ending M/C, leave an 12" end for fringe. Afghan is worked side to side.*

Body
Note: *Scrap color sequence is 10 different scrap colors indicated by letters A through J. Repeat colors in same sequence.*

With M/C, ch 239.

Row 1:
Working through BLs only, insert hook in 2nd ch from hook, YO and draw through, forming a lp on hook; * insert hook in next ch, YO and draw through; rep from * across—239 lps on hook. Slide all lps to opposite end of hook and turn work. Cut M/C.

Row 2:
To work lps off hook, with Color A make slip knot on hook; working from left to right, draw slip knot lp through first lp on hook; * YO, draw through 2 lps on hook (one of each color); rep from * until one lp remains on hook. Do not turn work.

Row 3:
Continuing with Color A and working right to left, ch 2, sk first vertical bar; (YO twice, insert hook under next vertical bar, YO and draw through, YO, draw through 3 lps on hook) 4 times; * † YO 3 times, sk next vertical bar, insert hook under next vertical bar, YO and draw through, YO, draw through 3 lps on hook †; (YO twice, insert hook under next vertical bar, YO and draw through, YO, draw through 3 lps on hook) 10 times; rep from * 18 times more, then rep from † to † once; (YO twice, insert hook under next

vertical bar, YO and draw through, YO, draw through 3 lps on hook) 4 times—239 lps on hook. Slide all lps to opposite end of hook and turn. Cut Color A.

Row 4:
Rep Row 2 with M/C.

Row 5:
Continuing with M/C and working right to left, ch 1, sk first vertical bar, (insert hook under next horizontal bar, YO and draw through) 4 times; * † YO twice, working behind rows, insert hook under next unused M/C vertical bar on 4th row below, YO and draw through, YO, draw through 3 lps on hook; sk next vertical bar †; (insert hook under next horizontal bar, YO and draw through) 11 times; rep from * 18 times more, then rep from † to † once; (insert hook under next horizontal bar, YO and draw through) 5 times. Slide all lps to opposite end of hook and turn. Cut M/C.

Row 6:
Rep Row 2 with Color B.

Row 7:
Continuing with Color B and working right to left, ch 2, sk first vertical bar, (YO twice, insert hook under next vertical bar, YO and draw through, YO, draw through 3 lps on hook) 10 times; * YO 3 times, sk next vertical bar, insert hook under next vertical bar, YO and draw through, YO, draw through 3 lps on hook, (YO twice; insert hook under next vertical bar, YO and draw through, YO, draw through 3 lps on hook) 10 times; rep from * across. Slide all lps to opposite end of hook and turn work. Cut Color B.

Row 8:
Rep Row 2 with M/C.

Row 9:
Continuing with M/C and working right to left, ch 1, sk first vertical bar, (insert hook under next horizontal bar, YO and draw through) 10 times; * YO twice, working behind rows insert hook under next unused M/C vertical bar on 4th row below, YO and draw through, YO, draw through 3 lps on hook; sk next horizontal bar, (insert hook in next horizontal bar, YO and draw through) 11 times; rep from * across. Slide all lps to opposite end of hook and turn work. Cut M/C.

Rep Rows 2 through 9 in following color sequence for scrap rows until piece measures about 45" ending by working a Row 4.

Color C
Color D
Color E
Color F
Color G
Color H
Color I
Color J
Color A
Color B

Next Row:

Continuing with M/C and working right to left, ch 1, sk first vertical bar, (insert hook under next horizontal bar, YO and draw through, YO, draw through both lps on hook) 4 times; * † YO twice, working behind rows, insert hook under unused M/C vertical bar on 4th row below, YO and draw through, YO, draw through 4 lps on hook; sk next horizontal bar †; (insert hook under next horizontal bar, YO and draw through, YO, draw through both lps on hook) 11 times; rep from * 18 times more, then rep from † to † once; (insert hook under next horizontal bar, YO and draw through, YO, draw through both lps on hook) 5 times.

Finish off and weave in scrap color ends.

Fringe

Following fringe instructions on page 6, make Single Knot Fringe. Cut 26" strands of M/C. For each knot use beginning or ending length on afghan plus 4 strands of M/C. Trim ends even.

Scrappy Squares

Size:
About 49" x 65"

Materials:
Worsted weight yarn, 36 oz (2520 yds, 1080 gms) M/C;
 17 oz (1190 yds, 510 gms) scraps
Note: *Our photographed afghan was made with*
36 oz (2520 yds, 1080 gms) off white (M/C) and
less than one skein each of 24 different colors.
Size K (6.5mm) double-ended crochet hook, or size
 required for gauge
Size I (5.5mm) regular crochet hook
Size 16 tapestry needle

Gauge:
one square = 8"

Instructions

Note: *Carry unused yarn along edge, twisting to*
avoid holes.

Square (make 48—2 squares each of 24 different colors**)**
With M/C, ch 24.

Row 1:
Working through BLs only, insert hook in 2nd ch from
hook, YO and draw through, forming a lp on hook;
* insert hook in next ch, YO and draw through; rep
from * across—24 lps on hook. Slide all lps to opposite end of hook and turn work. Do not cut M/C.

Row 2:
To work lps off hook, with scrap color make slip knot
on hook; working from left to right, draw slip knot lp
through first lp on hook; * YO, draw through 2 lps on
hook (one of each color); rep from * until one lp
remains on hook. Do not turn work.

Row 3:
Continuing with scrap color and working right to left,
ch 1, sk first vertical bar; * YO, sk next vertical bar,
insert hook between front and back bars of next vertical bar, YO, draw through; rep from * 10 times more;
insert hook between front and back bars on next vertical bar, YO and draw through—24 lps on hook. Slide
all lps to opposite end of hook and turn work. Do not
cut scrap color.

Row 4:
With M/C, YO and draw through one lp on hook; * YO,
draw through 2 lps on hook (one of each color); rep
from * until one lp remains on hook. Do not turn work.

Row 5:
Continuing with M/C and working right to left, ch 1,
sk first vertical bar; * insert hook under next vertical
bar, YO and draw through; insert hook under next
horizontal bar, YO and draw through; sk next vertical
bar; rep from * 10 times more; insert hook under next
vertical bar, YO and draw through—24 lps on hook.
Slide all lps to opposite end of hook and turn work.

Row 6:
Rep Row 4 with scrap color.

Row 7:
Continuing with scrap color and working right to left,
ch 1, sk first vertical bar, insert hook between front
and back bars of next vertical bar, YO and draw
through; * YO, sk next vertical bar, insert hook
between front and back bars of next vertical bar, YO
and draw through; rep from * across—24 lps on hook.
Slide all lps to opposite end of hook and turn work.

Row 8:
Rep Row 4.

Row 9:
Continuing with M/C and working right to left, ch 1,
sk first 2 vertical bars; * † insert hook under next horizontal bar, YO and draw through; insert hook under
next vertical bar, YO and draw through †; sk next
vertical bar; rep from * 9 times more, then rep from
† to † once; insert hook under next vertical bar, YO
and draw through—24 lps on hook. Slide all lps to
opposite end of hook and turn work.

Row 10:
Rep Row 6.

Rows 11 through 34:
Rep Rows 3 through 10 three times more.

Rows 35 through 40:
Rep Rows 3 through 8.

Row 41:
Continuing with M/C and working right to left, ch 1,
sk first vertical bar; * insert hook in next horizontal
bar, YO and draw through, YO, draw through both
lps on hook; rep from * across. Finish off.

Side Edging:
Hold square with one side edge at top; with M/C
make slip knot on regular hook and join with an sc in
end of first row in upper right-hand corner; work
21 sc evenly spaced across side—22 sc. Finish off.

Repeat on opposite side.

Square Edging

Hold piece with scrap color side most prominent facing you and Row 41 at top; join M/C in first st in upper right-hand corner, ch 2, in same st as joining work (dc, ch 2, 2 dc)—corner made; dc in next 22 sts, in next st work (2 dc, ch 2, 2 dc)—corner made; working along next side, dc in next 22 sc; working along next side in unused lps, in first lp work (2 dc, ch 2, 2 dc)—corner made; dc in next 22 lps; in next lp work (2 dc, ch 2, 2 dc)—corner made; working along next side, dc in next 22 sc; join in 2nd ch of beg ch-2.

Finish off and weave in all ends.

Assembly

With tapestry needle and M/C working through both lps, join blocks in 8 rows of 6 squares each. Sew rows together in same manner, working through both lps in a weaving motion.

Border

Hold afghan with one short end at top; with regular hook and M/C make slip knot on hook and join with an sc in upper right-hand corner ch-2 sp; 2 sc in same sp—corner made; sc in each dc to next ch-2 sp; † hdc in next ch-2 sp, dc in next joining, hdc in next ch-2 sp, sc in each dc to next ch-2 sp †; rep from † to † 4 times more; 3 sc in next corner ch-2 sp—corner made; sc in each dc to next ch-2 sp; rep from † to † 7 times; 3 sc in next corner ch-2 sp—corner made; sc in each dc to next ch-2 sp; rep from † to † 5 times; 3 sc in next corner ch-2 sp—corner made; sc in each dc to next ch-2 sp; rep from † to † 6 times; hdc in next ch-2 sp, dc in next joining, hdc in next ch-2 sp, sc in each dc to first sc; join in first sc.

Finish off and weave in ends.

Fiesta Fantasy

Size:
About 45" x 67"

Materials:
Worsted weight yarn, 24 oz (1680 yds, 720 gms) M/C;
   24 oz (1680 yds, 720 gms) scraps
Note: *Our photographed afghan was made with*
   24 oz (1680 yds, 720 gms) black (M/C) and less
   than one skein each of 9 different colors.
Size K (6.5mm) double-ended crochet hook, or size
   required for gauge
Size 16 tapestry needle

Gauge:
4 sts = 1"

Instructions

Body

Note: *Scrap color sequence is 9 different scrap*
colors indicated by letters A through I. Repeat colors
in same sequence.

With M/C, ch 180.

Row 1:
Working through BLs only, insert hook in 2nd ch from
hook, YO and draw through, forming a lp on hook;
* insert hook in next ch, YO and draw through; rep
from * across—180 lps on hook. Slide all lps to opposite end of hook and turn work.

Row 2:
To work lps off hook, with Color A make slip knot on
hook; working from left to right, draw slip knot lp
through first lp on hook; * YO, draw through 2 lps on
hook (one of each color); rep from * until one lp
remains on hook. Do not turn work.

Row 3:
Continuing with Color A and working right to left,
ch 1, sk first vertical bar; * sk next horizontal bar,
insert hook under next horizontal bar, YO and draw
through, ch 2, insert hook under next vertical bar, YO
and draw through; rep from * to last horizontal bar;
insert hook under last horizontal bar, YO and draw
through—180 lps on hook. Slide all lps to opposite
end of hook and turn work.

Row 4:
With M/C, YO and draw through one lp on hook; * YO
and draw through 2 lps on hook (one of each color);
rep from * until one lp remains on hook. Do not
turn work.

Row 5:
Continuing with M/C and working right to left, ch 1,
sk first vertical bar; * insert hook under next vertical
bar, YO and draw through, ch 2; insert hook under
next horizontal bar, YO and draw through; sk next
vertical bar; rep from * to last vertical bar, insert hook
under last vertical bar, YO and draw through—180 lps
on hook. Slide all lps to opposite end of hook and
turn work.

Row 6:
With Color A, YO and draw through one lp on hook;
* YO and draw through 2 lps on hook (one of each
color); rep from * until one lp remains on hook. Do
not turn work.

Row 7:
Continuing with Color A and working right to left,
ch 1, sk first vertical bar; * sk next horizontal bar,
insert hook under next horizontal bar, YO and draw
through, ch 2; insert hook under next vertical bar, YO
and draw through; rep from * to last horizontal bar;
insert hook under last horizontal bar, YO and draw
through—180 lps on hook. Slide all lps to opposite
end of hook and turn work.

Rows 8 through 11:
Rep Rows 4 through 7.

Rows 12 and 13:
Rep Rows 4 and 5.

Rows 14 through 21:
Rep Rows 2 through 9 using Color B on scrap rows.

Rows 22 through 25:
Rep Rows 2 through 5 using Color C on scrap rows.

Rep Rows 2 through 25 using scrap colors in following sequence until piece measures about 67" ending with a Row 4:
Color D
Color E
Color F
Color G
Color H
Color I
Color A
Color B
Color C

Next Row:
Continuing with M/C and working right to left, ch 1, sk first vertical bar; * insert hook under next vertical bar, YO and draw through, YO, draw through both lps on hook; insert hook undert next horizontal bar, YO and draw through, YO, draw through both lps on hook; sk next vertical bar; rep from * to last vertical bar; insert hook under last vertical bar, YO and draw through, YO, draw through both lps on hook.

Finish off and weave in ends.

Aurora Stripings

Size:
About 45" x 65"

Materials:
Worsted weight yarn, 17 oz (1190 yds, 510 gms) M/C; 25 oz (1750 yds, 750 gms) scraps
Note: *Our photographed afghan was made with 17 oz (1190 yds, 510 gms) off white (M/C) and less than one skein each of 15 different colors.*
Size K (6.5mm) double-ended crochet hook, or size required for gauge
Size I (5.5mm) regular crochet hook
Size 16 tapestry needle

Gauge:
13 sts = 3"

Instructions

Note: *Carry M/C along edge, twisting to avoid holes.*

Body

Note: *Scrap color sequence is 15 different scrap colors indicated by letters A through O. Repeat colors in same sequence.*

With M/C, ch 197.

Row 1:
Working through BLs only, insert hook in 2nd ch from hook, YO and draw through, forming a lp on hook; * insert hook in next ch, YO and draw through; rep from * across—197 lps on hook. Slide all lps to opposite end of hook and turn work.

Row 2:
To work lps off hook, with Color A make slip knot on hook; working from left to right, draw slip knot lp through first lp on hook; * YO, draw through 2 lps on hook (one of each color); rep from * until one lp remains on hook. Do not turn work.

Row 3:
Continuing with Color A and working right to left, ch 1, sk first vertical bar; * YO, (insert hook under next horizontal bar, YO and draw through) 3 times; lift 3rd lp on hook over next 2 lps slipping it off the hook; rep from * to last horizontal bar; insert hook under last horizontal bar, YO and draw through—197 lps on hook. Slide all lps to opposite end of hook and turn work. Cut scrap color.

Rows 4 and 5:
Rep Rows 2 and 3 with Color B.

Rows 6 and 7:
Rep Rows 2 and 3 with Color C.

Row 8:
Pick up M/C, YO and draw through one lp on hook; * YO and draw through 2 lps on hook (one of each color); rep from * until one lp remains on hook. Do not turn work.

Row 9:
Rep Row 3 with M/C.

Rep Rows 2 through 9, working in following color sequence on color rows until piece measures about 65" ending by working a Row 8.

Color D
Color E
Color F
Color G
Color H
Color I
Color J
Color K
Color L
Color M
Color N
Color O
Color A
Color B
Color C

Next Row:
Continuing with M/C and working right to left; * insert hook in next horizontal bar, YO and draw through, YO, draw through both lps on hook; rep from * across.

Border
Hold afghan with last row worked at top; join new scrap color in first st in upper right hand corner; ch 3, in same sp work (dc, ch 2, 2 dc) skip next 2 sts, † dc in next 3 sts, sk next st †; rep from † to † 47 times more; sk next st, in next st work (2 dc, ch 2, 2 dc); working along next side in edge of rows dc in each color to beg ch, working along lower edge in unused lps, in first lp work (2 dc, ch 2, 2 dc), sk next 2 lps, †† dc in next 3 lps, sk next lp ††; rep from †† to †† 47 times more; sk next lp, in next lp work (2 dc, ch 2, 2 dc); working along next side in ends of rows, dc in each color to beg ch-3; join in 3rd ch of beg ch.

Finish off and weave in ends.